WORLD'S FAIR
·NEW ORLEANS·

Photographs by Mitchel L. Osborne

The Official World's Fair Pictorial Book is a publication of Picayune Publishing, Inc., 920 Frenchmen Street, New Orleans, Louisiana, 70116, (504) 949-1366. Copyright © 1984, all rights reserved. Reproduction in whole or in part, without written permission, is strictly prohibited. Additional issues or bulk orders are available through Picayune Publishing, Inc.

Photography by Mitchel L. Osborne
Design by Margaret S. Boebel
Text by Jean W. Stastny
Production by Table 25
Printed by W. A. Krueger of America

ISBN number 0-937430-06-4

On the cover:
River god astride giant alligator greets visitors at the Bridge Gate.

The 1984 Louisiana World Exposition is a compendium of sights to dazzle the eye, sounds to delight the ear and tastes to tempt the palate. The whimsical, ever-changing Wonderwall, the colorful parades, the spectacular nightly fireworks are but a hint of the sights in store for the visitor. Musical treats ranging from classical opera to New Orleans jazz, from soul-stopping gospel to the Vienna Boys Choir will be performed continuously on the many stages located throughout the Fair site. And no one ever leaves the Fair hungry. Mouth-watering temptations from around the world will leave visitors wishing they had more than one stomach to fill.

Rivers of the World—Fresh Water as a Source of Life is the theme of the Fair. From May to November visitors will be treated to a tour of the four corners of the world to explore this theme and to celebrate this necessity of life. The tranquility of a Japanese water garden, the raging power of a white water Canadian river, the lushness of a Liberian rain forest and the life-giving waters of Egypt's Nile River can all be experienced during a visit to the 82 acre Fair site on the banks of the Mississippi River.

The water theme is carried throughout the Fair's six neighborhoods and begins at the spectacular entrance gates. The Bridge Gates are adorned by a giant river god and goddess astride 100 foot alligators. The City Gate's towering mermaids and water creatures beckon fairgoers to partake of the delights within their domain. Once inside, fairgoers can pick and choose their destination to one of the six neighborhoods, each with a different theme and character.

Louisiana alligator welcomes Fair visitors at the City Gate.

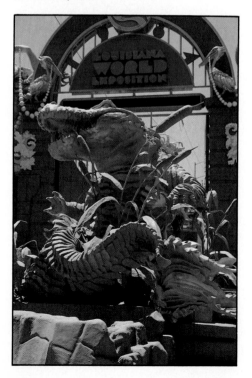

3

Empress Walk is reflected in Centennial Lagoon.

·CENTENNIAL PLAZA·

In recognition of the World's Industrial and Cotton Centennial Exposition held in New Orleans in 1884, Centennial Plaza portrays the charm and grace of the world of yesterday. Reflected in the splendid **Centennial Lagoon** is **Centennial Pavilion,** a group of seven separate modules which, when viewed from a specific vantage point, come together visually as a replica of the Main Building of the 1884 Cotton Centennial. A magnificent century old carousel gives visitors a ride into the past, while strains of John Philip Sousa and barbershop quartets may be heard coming from within the cooling confines of the **Frey Gazebo**.

But just as one is about to slip back into the ease and slower pace of the century past, the future appears in the form of a 20 story oil derrick atop the **Petroleum Industries Pavilion.** Centennial Plaza is also the neighborhood in which fairgoers board the **Mississippi Aerial River Transit (MART)** for a breathtaking gondola ride across the Mississippi River.

A classical statue supports a column of the Centennial Pavilion.

Right: A fanciful fish floats in Centennial Lagoon.

4

·THE INTERNATIONAL RIVERFRONT·

It is here in the giant Riverfront Pavilion that it can be truly said that "the world has come to New Orleans." Twenty-two countries are represented at the Louisiana World Exposition and visitors to the Fair will have the opportunity to learn of and experience the cultures of such diverse areas of the world as **Japan, Liberia** and **Australia**. **Korean** folk dancers perform the age old traditional movements of their native land while **Canada's** giant IMAX theatre transports visitors on a breathtaking journey through its magnificent countryside. The **United States** explores every facet of water and how it affects this country as **France, Egypt** and **Peru** explain how they have mastered their waterways through the ages. A close-up look at the space shuttle ENTERPRISE is provided by **NASA**. The International Riverfront is also the location of the **Amphitheatre** where many of the Fair's entertainment spectaculars take place.

Right: The exuberance of an African folk dance.

A Colonial altar done entirely in gold leaf graces the Mexico Pavilion.

An ancient Korean instrument is used to accompany folk dancers.

The Chrysler Pavilion showcases the state of the art technology utilized by the automotive industry.

Opposite Right: Fountains of all shapes and sizes grace the Watergarden.

· B A Y O U   P L A Z A ·

It is in Bayou Plaza that the water-related activity peaks at the Fair. The **Aquacade** features performances of synchronized swimming, water ballet, high diving and comedy routines in the first such event put together since the 1930's. **Watergarden** is a water wonderland where children and adults alike will get lost in the magic of the 14 intriguing fountains, games and displays which emphasize the fun and recreational uses of water. **Bayou Lagoon** with its rustic **Cajun Walk** will give fairgoers the opportunity to experience the peace and tranquility of strolling alongside a sleepy Louisiana bayou.

Chrysler and **Conergy** each sponsor exhibits in Bayou Plaza. From the high-tech world of automobile manufacturing to the "Energy Saving/Design Home of the Future," fairgoers will find these exhibits both interesting and informative. Steam locomotive No. 8444 will be a part of the **Union Pacific** exhibit which highlights the "Rivers of Steel" linking all parts of the United States.

Visitors are treated to a swimming and diving extravaganza at the Aquacade.

Water is once again the predominant theme in the 15 acre Great Hall where the **Water Course** showcases a floating extravaganza, a splendid bronze water sculpture embodies the spirit of the Fair and the **Louisiana Pavilion** takes visitors on a boat odyssey through make-believe swamps and bayous. A 110-foot steamboat, the RIVER ROAD QUEEN, rests on the tranquil waters of the **Water Course** and houses an exhibit spotlighting the Canadian province of Ontario and the 10 American states that lie along the Mississippi River. And the namesake of that river, the **State of Mississippi**, has also located its pavilion in the Great Hall where visitors can experience the ambiance and charm of the Magnolia State.

The Mississippi Pavilion focuses on the state's unique sights and sounds.

Man's thirst for God in his life is the theme of the Federation of Churches Pavilion.

Below: The Louisiana Pavilion takes visitors on a spectacular floating journey through the state.

· F E S T I V A L   P A R K ·

Giant puppets roam through the Italian Village to the delight of Fair visitors.

A more festive Festival Park would be hard to imagine. The **Italian Village**, a re-creation of an Italian piazza complete with shops, restaurants and entertainment, is alive with activity the whole day through. Moving to a more local, but no less lively beat is the **Jazz and Gospel Tent** where some of New Orleans' favorite music is heard. The magnificently restored **Federal Fibre Mills** building houses a **German Beer Garden, the Louisiana Folklife Festival** and **Jed's Lookout**, a third story lounge with a terrace providing a panoramic view of the action below. Not the least of **Federal Fibre Mills** tenants is the **monorail system** which has its starting point in the building. The ten car, air-conditioned train circles the Fair site, gliding past the International Riverfront and winding in and out of the Wonderwall. With convenient stops located throughout the Fair, it makes an excellent means of transporting fairgoers to all the wonderful sights, sounds and tastes they won't want to miss.

Above: The atmosphere
of the German Beer Hall
is enlivened by an
oom-pah-pah band.

The smooth riding
monorail offers the best
seat in the house for a
view of the entire Fair.

·FULTON STREET MALL·

A shopper's paradise, the **Fulton Street Mall** is a two block area carved from a once blighted warehouse district. Shops containing food and merchandise from all over the world give it the feeling of an international emporium. Roaming entertainers add to the festive marketplace atmosphere. **Reunion Hall**, the six month home base for New Orleans' own Pete Fountain, opens its doors with a jazz brunch and continues its spectrum of food and live entertainment into the early morning hours. The **Vatican Pavilion**, which houses treasures on loan from the Vatican musuem by special permission of Pope John Paul II, is one of the highlights of the Fair and a sight not to be missed.

Opposite Right: It's hard to stay seated when the great Pete Fountain begins playing at Reunion Hall.

The dome of the Vatican Pavilion is a focal point of Fulton Street Mall.

The world comes to
New Orleans on
the International River-
front.
Right: NASA's impres-
sive orbiter ENTERPRISE
stands guard over the
Mississippi River.
Below: Running the
length of the Interna-
tional Riverfront, Sky
Transpo offers great
views and a rest to
weary legs.

The impressive City Gates, designed and built by Barth Brothers, Inc., hint at the wonders within.
Left: A mythical sea god wrestles a giant alligator.
Right: Fetching mermaids beckon to visitors.
Below: A brown pelican, Louisiana's state bird, sits atop the City Gates.

Blaine Kern's Bridge Gates are both beautiful and a little bit scary. **Right:** Taming two fearsome alligators is no easy feat for King Neptune.

The theme of water begins at The Bridge Gates where sea gods, mermaids and water creatures join to greet Fair visitors.
Left: A smiling alligator lolls in the bayou beneath The Bridge Gates.
Below: Neptune and his lovely mermaid are framed by the Giant Wheel in Bayou Plaza.

Guaranteed to thrill and entertain, the amusement rides are a high point of any visit to the Fair.

Left: Soaring high over the Mississippi, the MART Gondola offers breathtaking views of the river, the city and the Fair.

Right: Your stomach stays 79 feet up in the air when the Rainbow platform suddenly drops back down to ground level.

Below Right: A trip along the Riverfront on Sky Transpo is a great way to see the magnificent ships that dock alongside the Fair.

The monorail is a convenient and unique means of transportation around the Fair's 82 acre site.

Right: Visitors can decide which treats they'll want to sample as they glide by on the monorail.

Circling the Fair in a counter clockwise direction, the air-conditioned, computer operated train takes 12 minutes to complete a round trip. **Above:** Far above the madding crowd, the monorail slips through Centennial Plaza.

Right: The high tech monorail presents a sharp contrast to the riverboat of days past.

Graced by cooling river breezes, the International Amphitheatre forms a spectacular staging area for some of the world's most famous performers.

Right: Kool & the Gang set the stage rocking.

Below: The Amphitheatre is a distinctive new landmark on the New Orleans skyline.

World class enter-
tainment will be
presented at the Amphi-
theatre during the six
month run of the Fair.
Right: Andy Williams
and **Below Right:** Lola
Falana project their own
special brands of magic
on the Amphitheatre
stage.

Opposite Page: A
graceful Korean dancer
performs a colorful folk-
dance.

Whimsical, wonderful water. Imaginations were let loose when it came to designing the Watergarden's Fountains. **Above:** A jumble of spinning balls, twirling circles and spouting water sprays come together to form this amusing fountain.
Left: What better theme for a water fountain than a refreshing fruit salad?

A stroll through the Watergarden in Bayou Plaza is a treat for young and old alike. **Right:** A water faucet and shower head prove that even these every day items can be transformed into a delightful fountain.

Concessions of every conceivable nature—from bubblegum snowballs to pizza-on-a-stick, from French porcelain to fish scale art—can be found throughout the World's Fair Site.
Left: A refreshing snowball is a welcome treat on a warm New Orleans afternoon.

Below: An indispensable purchase for every fairgoer—the **Official Guidebook** and the Official Map.
Right: Fantastic Faces paints more than just faces for the adventurous and daring fairgoer.

The spectacular Aqua-
quade offers water
ballet, synchronized swimming and high diving in
the first such live extravaganza produced since the
1930's.

Right: The clear, blue
waters of the Aquacade
pool provide the perfect
stage for the talented
swimmers and divers who
perform in the show.

Below: Enticing an
angry jungle god is the
fate of this hapless maid-
en in the hilarious south
seas episode of the Aqua-
cade performance.

Centennial Plaza evokes the charm and serenity of the 19th century while looking ahead to the future in the Electrical and Petroleum Industries Pavilions. **Right:** A 20 story oil rig towers above the Petroleum Industries Pavilion.

Revolving around Centennial Lagoon, Centennial Plaza is one of the six neighborhoods of the World's Fair.
Above: Aerial view of Centennial Plaza with the Amphitheatre in the background.

Right: The covered Empress Walk is the perfect spot to sit and enjoy the beauty of Centennial Lagoon.

The many attractions geared especially for children will delight youngsters of all ages.
Right: A run through the Kid Wash in Bayou Plaza is the best way around to wash off a sticky ice cream cone.
Below: Kids can test their water pistol accuracy at the target shoot in the Watergarden.
Opposite Page: The two mascots of the World's Fair, the debonaire pelican, Seymore D. Fair, and his charming alligator companion, roam throughout the site making guests young and old feel welcome.

A hodgepodge of architectural styles, the Wonderwall embodies all of the fantasy and imagination present in the 1984 World's Fair.
Right: Even a peacock blends into the colorful Wonderwall.
Opposite Page Top: At night the Wonderwall becomes even more fantastic as thousands of lights sparkle along its perimeter.
Opposite Page Bottom: A cherub atop the Wonderwall heralds the wonders of the Fair.

With all the charm and ethnic flavor of an Italian piazza, the Italian Village, strung with colorful lights and bunting and lined by restaurants and shops, will give fairgoers the feeling they're actually in the middle of Italy.

The sounds and smells are unmistakably Italian and the only problem is trying to decide which treat to sample next.

Left: Antipasto, pizza, spumoni—all the delicious flavors of Italy can be found in the Italian Village.

Below: He may not look Italian, but he's still having fun at the Italian Village.

The ships of many nations can be seen in this Fair which celebrates the great water ways of the world.
Left: Although only one-third the size of the original, this Korean turtle ship is still an impressive sight.
Right: A delicate sampan stands at the entrance to the China Pavilion.
Below Right: The U.S. Coast Guard's tall ship EAGLE regally stands guard over the Mississippi Riverfront.

Every evening at 10:30 the skies over the Mississippi come alive in a spectacle of light and sound as a magnificent display of fireworks signals the end of another exciting day at the World's Fair.
Right: The dancing fountains of Centennial Lagoon mirror the fireworks above.
Below: The entire Fair is awash with the colorful show in the skies.
Opposite Page: Fireworks illuminate the Giant Wheel.